Normee Ekoomiak

ARCTIC MEMORIES

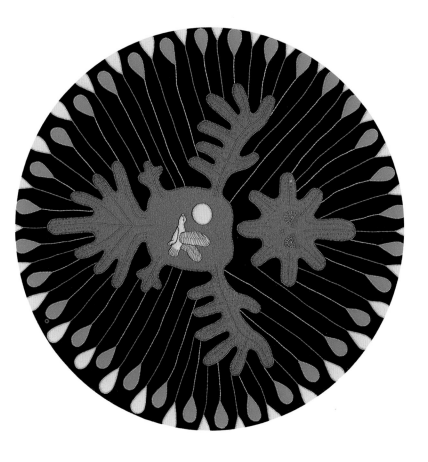

NC Press Limited · Toronto

Thanks to Lillian Robinson, Dr. Brian Dobbs, Bela Kalinovits, Phil Surguy, Leo Flaherty, Rolf Roemer, Katolic Utatnaq, the Baffin Divisional Board of Education, the Ontario Arts Council, the Canada Council and the Multiculturalism Sector of the Department of the Secretary of State without whose help this book would never have been published.

New Canada Publications, a division of NC Press Limited, Box 452 Station A, Toronto, ON, Canada M5W 1H8

Printed in U.S.A.

Revised edition, 1989
© Normee Ekoomiak, 1988

Canadian Cataloguing in Publication Data

Ekoomiak, Normee, 1948-
    Arctic Memories

2nd ed. rev.
Text and t.p. in English and Inuktitut.
ISBN 1-55021-059-9

1. Inuit—Pictorial works.* I. Title.

N6549.E56A2 1989   970.004'97   C89-090576-2

ARCTIC MEMORIES

Who I Am

I am an Inuk.

My people are the Inuit of James Bay in Arctic Quebec. My father's people came from the country around Povungnituk. My mother's family came from Great Whale River. Right across the water are our cousins on the Belcher Islands. We call ourselves "Inuit," which means "people." Our neighbors, the Cree Indians, call us "Eskimos." This means "people who eat raw fish."

On April 19, 1948, while my family was in its spring camp, traveling to meet Indian friends at Fort George, which we now call Chisasibi, I was born in a place of magic: at Cape Jones. This is where James Bay empties into Hudson Bay, on the east shore, the Quebec side. Across the water, on the Ontario shore to the west, is Cape Henrietta Maria, which is called for the wife of the King of England who gave permission to start the Hudson's Bay Company and to trade with the Inuit and to be our friends.

I can remember everything. I grew up at Fort George in my grandfather's tent, which had a wooden frame and was covered in canvas and with seal skins. It was about ten feet by twenty feet. I lived there with my grandfather, who taught me everything, and with my father and mother and with my six brothers and my seven sisters. I went to school at the mission there.

When I was a baby, only six months old, I did not stop crying. My mother wanted to know what kind of sickness I had, but I wasn't sick. I was still crying so they took me to the church and a very great and holy man, the Bishop Marsh, baptized me and the Spirit went into me and I stopped crying and I looked at the man and I smiled. Before I was a year, I found out that I had special powers. I was able to go through walls and walk in the air and go to different places. I knew all of the spirits of the land animals and the birds and the fish and the sea animals. I knew their names and I could understand them and I could speak to them. I have heard the owl and I have heard the bear and I have heard the Sedna singing. When I was small, I had a sickness in my ears and it did not go away properly. So now it is hard for me to hear what other people are saying, but I can still hear the spirits.

Now I will show you some of my art, my paintings and my wall hangings. Then I will tell you about what has happened to me when I came to the South.

—text prepared by Dr. Brian Dobbs

NORMEE EKOOMIAK.

ᐃᒡᓗ ᐅᓗᐊᓂ

ᓄᑕᕋᕈᓗᒃᖢᖓ ᐃᒡᓗᒥᒐᓛᕆᐊᓕᐅᕐᕕᒋ ᐅᑭᐅᕐᕕᐅᑎᓪᓗᒍ
ᐄᓗ ᐅᑭᐅᕈᓘᔪᖅ ᐃᓂᖃᖅᑐᑎᑦ ᑐᐱᕐᒥᐊᑎᓪᓗᒍ.
ᐅᑭᐅᖃᐃᑦᑐᒥ ᓯᕿᓂᖃᖅᑐᑎ ᐅᑭᐅᕐᒥᒃ, ᐊᖅᑭᑦᓴᖅᓗ
ᐄᓗ ᑕᐊᒃᑐᓂ. ᖃᓐᖑᒃ ᑕᐅᒃᑐᕐᑐᑦ ᐊᑐᐊ
ᐅᑭᐅᒐᓚᐃᖅᑐᑎ ᐅᑭᐅᕐᒥᒃ. ᕿᒪᒃᖢᓗᖓ ᑖᑦᓲᑦ
ᐅᐱᐊᖃᒥᐊᕈᓗᑎᑦ ᐊᓇᓇᒻᒪᕋᑦᓴᓕᐅᕆᐊᓕᖅᑑᑯ
ᐊᓇ ᖃᐅᒪᔪᓕᖅᑐᖅ ᐊᑖᑕ ᐊᑐᐊᓐᐊᓇᕐᓇᓐᓇᖅ. ᐅᑭ
ᐄᓗ ᕿᒪᒃᖢᓂᐊᓂ ᑕᐊᖅᑐᑕᐊ ᐊᑎᕐᕕᐊᑦ ᑕᐊᒃᑐᕐᒥᒃᑎᓐᓇ.
ᕿᐊᐃᑦ ᐊᒥᓂᒃ ᑕᐊᖅᑐᖅᑐᑕ ᐊᖑᓇᑕᐊ ᑕᐊᖅᑐᑦ,
ᓄᑦᖃᔅᖢᖓ ᐊᒡᓗ ᐅᖅᑯᒥᓇᑐᑕ ᑕᐊᓐᖓᐅ ᑕᐊᖅᑐᑦ
ᐅᑑᒪᔪᓐᖑᕐᒥᑐ, ᖃᕆᑕᕐᓯᓐᖢᒍᑐᕿ ᐊᓇᖅᑯᑦ ᑖᒐᐄ
ᐄᒃᓕᖅᑎᕐᓇᑐ ᐅᓇᒍᖅᖢᑐ ᐊᖑᓇᒃᖢᕐᒋ ᐊᖑᖅᑖᓕ

In the Iglu

"Iglu" means house. When I was small, we used to live in a snow house in the winter and in a tent the rest of the year. During the long winter up North, there is little sun and it is always dark. We stay inside and do our work and play. Here the father is carving a soapstone sculpture for sale at the co-op. The mother is sewing together seal skins to cover a tent. When it starts to get warm, the snow house will melt. We will build a tent to live in, and we will move with it from place to place when we hunt for food. Inside the iglu there is an oil lamp on three legs. It is for light and for heat. But when we go to sleep, we put out the lamp, and then it gets cold, so we must all sleep together to keep warm. The kids sleep in the middle, between their parents.

ᐃᑭᐅᕐᒥᐅᑐᒥ ᐅᐱᕐᖓᒥ

ᑐᖑᓱᓕᕐᖓᓕᕐᑐᑦ ᐊᒻᒪᓗ ᑕᑕᐅᖃᒃᑲᐅᑦᑎᐊᑐᑦ ᕆᓈᖅᓴᕐᔫᒃ. ᑕᖕᒐᕐᕕᐅᑦ ᑐᕆᕈᓕᑐᑖᑕᖏᑦ ᐅᐱᕐᖓᒃᑭᐊᖅ
ᐊᔾᔨᒋᐊᖅᐅᑖᕐᓂᓱ, ᑕᖕᒐᕐᕕᐅᑦ ᐅᖃᖅᕈᓪᓕᐊᑕᕈᓕᑕᕆᖃᐅᐱᐅ ᑎᖓᐅᖃᖅᕕᐊ ᐸᓪᓕᑕᑕᐊᑎᖓᓐ ᐸᕕᑖᓗᒃᖓᖅ
ᐱᑕᖅᕆᓱᑕᑦ. ᓯᓐᓂᖑᑐᑦ ᑕᕐᓯᕿᑦ ᐊᒻᒪᓗ ᐃᐱᕋᕋᓗᕕᓕᕈᒥᖕ.

ᓇᓄᖅ ᓂᖕᑐᖃᕈᒃ ᓂᖃᕈᕐᑐᑖᑐᑦ. ᐊᓇᓇᖅᒥᖕ ᓇᒻᓯᒃᕐᖓᑐᑦ ᐃᖅᖏᐅᑎᓈᕈᖃᐅᑕ ᑕᕐᕋᐅᖅᕈᑕᑕᐅᖕ ᓇᓄᖓᓄᕐᖓᐅᑕ
ᐃᐅᒥᕝᕈᑕᕐᕈᐊᕐᓂᐅ. ᓂᖅᖓ ᓇᑕᑦᑐᖃᐅᑕᕋᖓ ᓇᒃᕈᖃᐱᖅᕋᑐ ᕆᕋᐱᖃ ᐊᒃᕋᕈᐊᑦ ᐊᕐᕈᖃᖅᕋᑦᖓᖃ
ᐊᒪᖅᕈᑐᑕᖓ ᐅᐃᕋᐊᕈ.

Arctic Spring

The ice is breaking up, getting ready to float across James Bay. It will soon be summer, and the Canada geese are flying north to lay eggs to make more Canada geese. If they are born in the South, they are not as healthy. There is too much pollution, and they do not have the right food. They like the North because it's natural for them.

Nanook, the polar bear, is hungry and is looking for food. The mother seal calls the baby seal, and they swim away and are safe. Now the bear has to eat fish. He would like to eat seal, but if he eats too much of it, he will get wild. It is better for bears to eat fish most of the time. Then they can be our friends.

ᖁᓕᒃᑕᓂᑦ ᐊᑎᐅᕕᐸᓂᕐᒥ

ᕿᐱᓗᒍᓚᑕᐃᑦᑎᔪᑎᑦ ᓱᓕᓇᒥ. ᑕᑕ ᐊᒐᓯᑎ ᖁᑎᖃᑕᐅᔪᑦ
ᐸᖓᓱᓂᒃ ᐊᖁᓪᓕ ᐱᖅᑯᒥᖃ ᐃᓱᒃᓱᓇᓗᐊᓕᖅ.
ᕈᓂᒥ ᖁᑎᖃᑕᐅᔭᓕᒃ ᓂᐆᕐ ᐊᐃᓄᓐᖁᓴᑦᖓᖑᒋ ᖁᑎᖃᑕᐅᔪᓄᓯᓐ ᓂᒪᑎ
ᐃᓱᖑᓯᐊᓂᐆᕐ.

ᐃᑐᐆᒍ ᐹᑕᕿᑦᕿᐅᐃ ᑐᑐᐊᐆ ᐊᔪᓛᓇ.
ᐱᓄᕐᐆᓇᖁᖁᒡᖁᓂᑦ ᐆᑐᐊᕿᕐᓯᓄᒍ ᖁᖃ ᖁᐃᖃᓐ ᐆᐆᓴᓂᒐᑦ.

Playing on a Snowbank

We love to go outside and play. Here three boys and a girl are playing with their father on a snowbank. They all slide down, and then race to get back to the top and do it all over again.

Inside an iglu there is not very much space. You cannot stay inside for a long time, not even during a snowstorm. But if you go outside to play, then your body will always be healthy and normal.

Also, someone has to go outside the iglu after a snowstorm to dig the people out.

NORMEE EKOOMIAK

ᒥᑯᒋ ᐃᖅᑲᓈᐱᖅᓂᖅ

ᐃᓄᓇᓂᒃᐳᒃ ᐱᖅᑐᐊᓈᖃᖅᓄᑦ ᐅᒪᒃᒃ ᑕᖅᓄᐊ ᑐᖅᓄᐊᑦ, ᓄᒃᒃ
ᐊᖢᒃᒃ ᐊᑕᐅᓂᒃ ᓄᐊᖃᖅ ᐊᖅᓴᓄᖃᖅᑐᐊᒃ, ᓄᖅᐱᓄᖅᓴᒃᑐ
ᑭᒃᐊᓄ ᐱᖃᖅᓄᖅᓱᓴᐱᖅ ᐊᖅᓵᖅᓱᖅᐱᖅᖅᑐᒃ, ᓄᖅᐊᐃᓄᖃᖅᓴᑐᐊᑦᐅ
ᐊᖅᓂᐊᖅᐃᖅᐅᖅᓴᑕᐅᑐᖅᐱᔾᑦ ᐊᖅᓴᑐᓴᖅᓴᖅᑐᓂᖅ ᐊᖅᓴᓄᖅᑐᖅᓄ.

ᐊᖅᓄᓴᑐ ᑕᑲᐱᓴᔾ ᐊᐃᓄᓴᑦ ᑯᓂᐊᖅᖅ
ᐊᖅᓴᑐᖅ ᐊᖅᓴᖅᓄᐊᖅᓴᖅᐊᖅᖅᓴ ᑯᖅᐊᐅᒃ ᐊᖅᓴᓄᖃᖅᒃ
ᐊᖅᓴᖅᑐᓈᓄᖅᐊᖅᓄ.

ᐲᓴᖅᓂᖅᖅᐊᖅᓄᑯᖅᓴᖅ ᓴᖅᓄᑕᑯᖅᓴᖃᐅᓴᑲᓴᖅᓂᖅᓴᓂ ᓄᑯᖅ
ᑐᓴᑯᖅᐱᖅᓄ ᐊᖅᓴᑯᖅᓴᑐᖅᓴᖅᓂᔾᐅᑐᑦ, ᐊᖅᓴᑐᑲᖅᓴᔾ ᒥᖅᓴᓄᖅᓴᖅᓄᖅ
ᖅᐅᖅᓴᑭᐊᑯᐅᑐᑦ ᓄᐊᖃᓴᖅᓂᖅᓴ ᐅᒪᖅᓄᐊᖅᓴ.

Ice Fishing

After a snowstorm it is hard to find caribou and seal and walrus. All of the birds and animals are gone. Sometimes months go by before they come back. So the whole family has to go out fishing, to catch the arctic char, through holes in the ice. Sedna is good, and she makes sure there are plenty of fish. But sometimes it is hard to catch any fish, and the birds and animals stay away for a long time. Then the people must move to a new camp if they are strong enough. Or else they will starve.

ᐅᑭᕙᐃ - ᖁᕕᐊᕈ

ᐃᕕᐃᒃ ᐅᖃᖅᑕᐅᔪᒥᒃ ᐃᓄᖕᓄ. ᑕᐃᓇ ᐃᓚᓐᓄᕋᔭᕗᑦ ᐊᖁᖅᑲᑖᑦᑎᑦ ᒥᕐᓇᖏᓐᓄ ᐃᓄᐃᑦ ᐊᖅᑲᖁᑖᖅᑕᐅᔮᖅᑲᐅᔭᖓ ᐅᒪᔪᓕᕆᓂᕐᒧᑦ. ᐃᓪᓗᖓ ᑕᐃᑉᑯᐊ ᐃᕝᕕ ᐊᖅᑲᖁᑖᖅ ᓯᕿᓂᕐᒥᒃ, ᑕᖅᑭᒥᒃ ᐊᒻᒪᓗ ᐅᓪᓗᕆᐊᑦ. ᐊᖁᖅᑖᖅᑕᐅᔪᖅ ᐊᑖᑕᒥᒃ ᐊᖑᓇᓱᒃᑐᒥᒃ ᖃᐃᒻᒥᒥᒃ ᑲᐱᔾᔪᑎᒥᓪᓗ ᓇᖑᓂᖓᒃ, ᐊᒻᒪᓗ ᓇᐃᒻᒪᑦᑎᐊᖅᑐᖅ ᐊᓈᓇᒥᒃ ᓄᑕᕋᖃᖅᑐᒥᒃ ᐊᒪᐅᑎᒥᓂ. ᐃᒃᐱᓕᐊ ᐊᖁᖅᑖᖅᑕᐅᔪᖅ ᐅᒥᖓ ᐃᑭᓕᓂᖅ ᐊᒻᒪᓗ ᓂᕐᓕᐊᑦ. ᐃᓗᐃᑦᑐ ᐅᒪᔪᓕᕆᓂᕐᒥᒃ ᐊᖁᖅᑎᒋᔪᑦ ᐃᖏᕐᕋᓕᖅᑲᐅᔭᖅᑐᑦ ᑕᐃᓇ ᐃᑉᑯᐊᑐᐊᖅ ᐃᓄᐃᑦ ᐊᖁᖅᑎᒋᔮᖅᑎᒃ ᐊᓇᖁᑦᑎᐊᖅᑕᐅᔪᑦ.

Okpik—The Lucky Charm

"Okpik" means "snowy owl." He is our friend, and his spirit protects all of nature in the North. Here you see the owl spirit, with the sun and the moon and the stars. He is watching over a father who is going hunting with his dog and spear, and he is watching over a mother with a baby in the hood of her *amautiq*. Okpik also is the guardian of the polar bear and of the geese. All of the nature spirits work together and watch over the North. We must keep them happy and only kill the right animals or else the spirits will not let us find food.

ᓂᒋ   ᐊᐃᒃᑎᓇᐊᖅᓲᑕᖕ

ᐃᓪᕐᑦᕁᑕᖕ ᐱᐃᐃᔾᕐᕑᕐᖄ. ᐃᓕᕆᖅᑕᑕ ᓂᖅᖅᓄᖅᕁᕆᖅᑎᓇᓄ. ᑕᒪᑦᑦ
ᓄᓇᑦᐊᖅᑕᖕ>ᔾ ᐱᒍᑦ ᑐᐱᑦᐊᑨᓗ ᖅᕐᕁᕆᖅᖄ ᐊᕐᐊᕁᓂ, ᒪᔾᖄᖄᒃ ᐊᕿᖅᑎᓄ. ᓇᐸᐊᓄᐊᑦ
ᐊᓇᐊ ᐊᐃᐊᔷᕁᕑᓂᖅ ᑦᒪᓄ ᓇᖅᓇᒪᓪᓱᓄᖅ ᐃᓄᔾᐃᓇᐃᖅᖕᕁᓄᒃ, ᓇᔾᖄᐊᑦ ᐊᓄᖅᐊᕁᑦ ᐃᖅᖄᓄᑎᕁ
ᓂᓕᖓᓇᕁᔾᖕᓄ ᐊᕁᕁᓇᖅᑕᓪᑦ ᐊᕐᓄᖅᓄᕁᓇ ᐃᒪᓄᕁᒦᕁᒦ.

ᐃᓪᕐᑦᕁᑕᖕ ᐅᕁᐅᓄᑦ ᐊᕁᕁᔾᕑᓕᑦᕁᖅᑎᓇᐊᕐᓪᖄ: ᖃᓂᑦᖃᕁᓄᕁᓇ, ᑦᕑᕁᖅᖕᕁᓄ ᐊᕁᓗ
ᓇᓇᕁᕑᖅᖕᕁᓄᒃ. ᐊᓄᐊᐊᑦ ᐊᕁᓇᐊᓄᕁᑦᖕᓗᕁ ᐊᐃᕁᕁᓇᕁᑦᕁᖅᖕᒃ ᓇᒋᐊᐃᐊᕁ. ᑕᐊᓄᖅᕁᖕᑦ ᐃᓄᐊᑦ
ᔾᓄᕑᐊᑦ ᖅᖄᕁᖓᕁᕑᓄᒃ ᐃᖅᖅᖅᔾᕐᕑᕁᖅᑐᕁᑦ.

The Body Needs to Travel

This happened a long time ago. There was no food near the village. The people had to travel to a new place, miles and miles across the ice of Hudson Bay. Half of the people did not want to go. They wanted to stay where they were born and grew up. But the other people said the body needs to travel. They had to find the right spot for themselves, where there would be more animals and birds and fish.

This took place thousands of years ago. There was no Canada and no Arctic Quebec and no Northwest Territories. This was how the Inuit went from one place to all of the other places. This is why all of the people who live around the North Pole can understand each other and why they speak languages that are almost the same.

ᐱᓯᒡᓕ ᐊᑦ

ᐃᐃᓴᖃᒃᐳᑦ ᐊᖏᒡ ᐋᒡᐹᒡᒥᕈ ᐊᓚᑲ ᐊᖃᐊᕐ ᐊᓪᒃᐸᖅ,
ᓚᖃᖆᖅᐳᖅ. ᐸᔅᓛᖃᐱᑕᕿᐅᓚᐅᑦ ᓵᐊᖃᖆᐸᑎᑦᖑᑕ ᐊᖅᐲᐊᐱ
ᖃᑎᐊᒐ ᐊᕐᒃᒃᓚᒃᑲᑕᒃ ᓚᑦᖃᐊᕐᓛᕐᐱᑎᑕᖅᒃ
ᐊᕈᖆᖃᑐᕐᑲᓐᑕᕝᐱᖅ ᐋᓛᖅ ᓴᖃᖆ, ᓐᐊᒃᖃ ᖁᒪᕈᖅ ᐊᐱᖃᐊ
ᑎᑎᓚᓇᕐᒃᖅᕝ.

ᒪᖅᕋᖆᓐ ᐃᐅᐱᑦ ᑕᑲᐲᖅ ᖅᐊᖆᖅ ᖃᐄᓛᕐᖅ
ᐊᔅᓇᖃᕈᐱᖃᑎᑎᓯ ᐊᖅᐲᖃᑲᖃᐊ ᐃᑎᐲᑕᖆᐸᑎᑦᒃ
ᐊᓯᒪᕐᖃᖅᒃᒃᖅᑕᐱᐅᑦᒃ ᐋᓛᒃ ᕿᐲᐊᖆ ᓴᕆᐊᕐᒐᑕᕝᑕ.

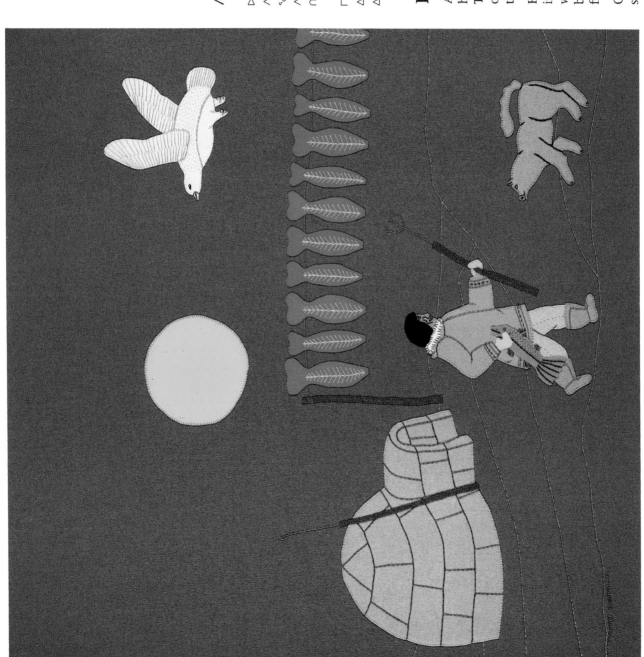

Hanging Fish

After the fish have been caught, the people have to hang them up to dry and to freeze. They cannot leave the fish under the snow, or the polar bear or wolf or fox could find the fish and eat it.

Here the snowy owl sees the polar bear coming and warns the people. They take the fish with them inside the iglus and wait for the bear to go away. Then they will hang the fish up again.

Okpik watches over his people and makes sure that their food is safe.

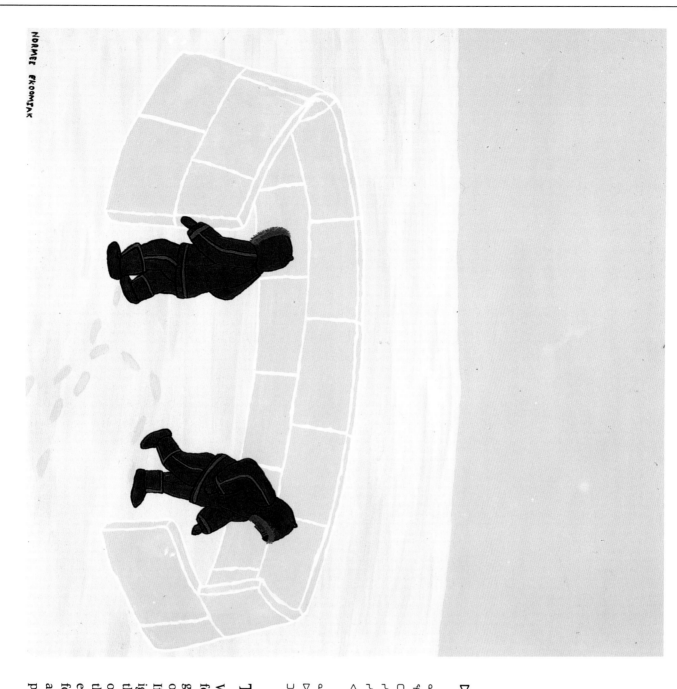

NORMEE EKOOMIAK

ᐁᒡᐅᐃᖅ

ᓇᓂᓯᔪᒥᓇᖕᒋᓐᓂᖅ ᓄᒐᖕᖏᔪᕐᖃᓕᖅᐸᑦ ᐊᕐᕕᓗᒃᓄᐊᕚᖓᔪᑦ
ᖃᓄᕐ᠊ᐸᕐᑐᐃᑦ ᐊᖑᓇᓱᕐᒃᓇᐊᕚᕐᓇᖐᓇ᠊ᖓᓂ᠊
ᓴᖕᒪᑐᐊᓇᖃᓴᖐᖅᓂᖅ ᐊᖐᓇᐊᕐᐸᕚᓇᒃᓂᖅ
ᐸᕐᒪᐅᕐᔭᕐᒃᑕᐊᑎᖐᖕᒐᖐᓇᓇ ᐊᕐᓄᓄᕚᐊᕐᑐᑐᖐᖐᕐᖃ, ᐸᕐᐊᐊᖐᓇ
ᕐᓇᐅᖐᕚᕐᕕᖐᕐᖃᖐᕐᑭ ᐅᕐᖐᐊᐃᓇ᠊ᐅᑐᐊᓇᓄᖐᖅᐅᓂᖅ ᐸᕐᐊᕐᔪᓇ
ᐊᕚᕐᓂᕐᖐ᠊

ᓇᓇᕐᕚᕐᖃᐅᕐᒐᓕᓪᖐᖅ ᑐᐃᑭᕐᒃᕐᕿᕚᒐᓇᖅ ᐅᑎᕿᐊᑕ ᐊᓕᕐ᠊ᓄ
ᐅᕐᖃᑎ ᐊᐅᑎᓄᕐᕐᖐᖐᒐ ᒪᓇᓇᐃᖐ ᑕᐃᓇᓇᕐᖅ ᐊᓇᓇᕐᑭᓇᓇ
ᑐᐃᐸᕐᒃᑎᓇᕐᔭᓇᕿ᠊᠊

The Shelter

When it is hard to find animals and fish for food, then the two best hunters in the village go out to look for a better place. At the end of the day, they build a shelter for the night. If the weather is bad, they build a whole iglu. But when the weather is not bad, all they need is a windbreak made of two layers of snow blocks. At the end of the next day they build another shelter. This goes on every day until the hunters find a good spot for a new village. Then they go back home, and soon the other Inuit, ten or twenty people, will move to a new place.

ᐱᕐᓗᒃᑕᐅᓯᒪᔪᐃᑦ

ᑕᐃᑉᓱᒪᓂᒎᖅ ᑕᐃᒃᑯᐊ ᐃᓄᓱᒃᑐᐃᑦ ᖃᐅᔨᔭᐅᕙᒥᒃ ᐱᔭᕇᐊᖅᑲᐅᖏᑕᒥᓂᑦ. ᐃᓕᕆᓱᓕᕆᒥᒃ ᐱᕐᓗᒃᑕᐅᓯᑎᓕᕐᐳᑦ. ᑕᒃᑯᐊ ᐃᓄᓱᒃᑐᐃᑦ ᐃᑭᑉᓗᑎᒃ ᐅᒥᐊᕐᒥᑦ ᐊᒻᒪᓗ ᐅᖓᓯᒃᑐᒧᑦ ᐃᖏᕐᕋᑉᓗᑎᒃ ᓯᕿᓂᖕᒥᐅᒧᑦ. ᓄᓇ ᑕᑯᔪᓐᓇᐃᓕᕐᕗᒍ ᑭᓯᐊᓂ ᐊᑯᓐᕐᑐᐃᓐᓇᕐᓂᑦ ᑕᐅᑐᙵᓐᓇᕐᓗᑎᒃ. ᑕᒃᑯᐊ ᐃᒋᕗᓂᒃᑐᒃ ᐸᐅᑎᖏᑦ, ᓂᕿᖏᑦ ᐊᒻᒪᓗ ᐊᓯᖏᓪᓗ ᐱᕐᑯᑎᖏᑦ ᐃᒪᕐᒧᑦ. ᓇᓂᔭᐅᑉᓗᑎᒃ ᐱᖓᓱᓂᑦ ᐱᓇᓱᐊᕈᓰᑦ ᖃᖏᕋᒪᑦ, ᑐᕐᖁᖓᓗᒃᑳᕐᓗᑎᒃ ᑳᖏᓂᑯᒧᑦ.

The Curse

This is a true story. When an evil person learns your name, he can use your name when he does bad things. This is a terrible curse.

Once, some teenage boys went to school in the South. A bad man discovered their names, and then he committed crimes. The police came to arrest the boys and did not believe they were not guilty. So the boys went to jail for something they had not done. When they got out, they were sent back home. They told their parents what had happened. They had been beaten up and sent to jail. This was a terrible scandal and a shame and a curse.

So the boys had to die. They got into an *umiak* and went out into James Bay so far that they could no longer see the land but only the waves. Then they threw their paddles and their food and oil and their warm clothing over the side of the boat. They were found three weeks later. They had all starved to death.

NORMEE EKOOMIAK

ᓇᑉᓯᖃᖅᑐᖅ ᐃᖅᑭᑎ ᐃᖅᐸᒌᓐᖑ

ᐃᓄᐃᑦ ᖁᐱᕐᔪᐊᖅᓂᒃ ᐊᖅᓯᐅᐊᖁᒥᑦ ᓄᖅᑕᒃᖅᑕ ᐊᖅᓯᖅᑕᐅᖃᑦ
ᐊᕆᓗᓄ ᐃᓐᑎᐅ ᐃᔅᓄ ᖃᑕᐅᓯᔅᑎᑦ, ᖁᑭᖅᒧᕐᖔᖅ
ᐃᖅᐸᓯᒄ ᐊᖅᓚᑖᐅᔥᖓ ᓇᐊᔨᖅᑖ ᖁᔪᖅᓴᖃᑎᐅᐊᖅᓄᐊᖅᓂᓱ
ᐲᔩᐊᓯᒐ ᖃᑕᖅ ᐃᓄᖅ ᔭᑎᐅᔾᑖᖃᔥᖁᑉ ᐊᐅᓴᖅ, ᑕᐃᓪ ᖃᑕᖅ
ᐃᓱᖅ ᓴᓇᓯᔥᖅᑎᖓ.

ᖃᑕᖅ ᐃᓄᖅᐸᑖᑐᒄ ᖃᓐᑖᑐᖅ ᖁᐱᖅᑯᐊᖅᑕᐊᖅᓯᒃ, ᑕᐃᕐᓄ
ᖁᔪᑖᐅᔨᒃᓯᐱᑖᑖᖃᖅ ᖄᕐᓴᖃᑑᖅᒃᖓᔥᖓ.

High-Kick Game

When there is a lot of food and there is nothing else to do, the Inuit make up games to play.

In the high-kicking game, the pole is raised higher and higher until only one person can kick the ball. That person is the winner. Another boy is playing the hopping game. Here you hop for as long as you can. This is a contest, and whoever hops the longest wins. The other boy is doing a push-up and trying to pick a stick up with his mouth. His body must not touch the ground.

These games are fun, but they also make the body strong.

ᕿᐱᖕᒍᑦ ᐃᒋᑦᑕᕐᑕᐅᓂᖅ

ᕿᐱᖕᒍᑦ ᐃᒋᑦᑕᕐᑕᐅᓂᖅ ᖁᕕᐊᓇᕐᑐᖅ. ᑕᒃᑯᐊ ᑕᓐᓇ ᓂᕕᐊᕐᓵᕐᔪᒃ ᕿᐱᖕᒍᑦ ᐃᒋᑦᑕᕐᑕᐅᔪᖅ. ᐊᓄᓚᒃᑲᓪᓚᒃᑐᖅ ᓄᔭᕐᒥᓄᑦ. ᑕᓐᓇ ᕿᑎᒍᓯᖅ ᓄᑕᕋᓄᑦ ᐱᒍᑦᑎᓐᓇᖅᑐᖅ ᑭᓯᐊᓂ ᖁᕕᐊᓇᕈᑕᐅᑐᐃᓐᓇᕐᑐᖅ.

Blanket-Toss Game

Blanket tossing is great fun. Here a girl is being tossed up in the air. The wind is blowing through her long hair. This game makes the children stronger, but it is just for fun, to have a good time.

ᐊᓗᒥ ᕐ

ᐃᓄᐃᑦ ᐊᔭᐅᐱᓕᑦᑕᐅᖁᐊᓂ ᓕᓇᑐᐱᐊᖕᓂ ᐊᖕᓗ ᐅᓕᕐᔪᕈᖕᓂ ᐊᖃᓯᖕᓂ ᑕᐅᖗ ᐊᖕᓕᒥ
ᐊᖓᐅᐊᖅᐊᐃ ᖅᕿᓯᖁ 22-ᖂᓗᖏᓴ ᐊᖂᐅᐱᓂ ᑭᖅᐊᓴ ᐊᖂᓕᐅᑕᐃ ᐱᐊᓕᓇ ᖓᖕᐊᑐᐃ
ᐊᑐᓴᐃᐊᖁᐊᔪᐃᐅ ᐱᐊᓴᐅᕗᑦᕈᖅ 200-ᓴ ᐊᖅᐃᖏᐅᑐᐃ ᖃᓴᐅᐃᑐᐅᐊᖃᓯᖂ ᐊᒥ ᖃᕿᓴᖕᖏ
ᐊᖂᑕᖃᓯᖂ.

The String Game

The Inuit like to make figures of things and animals with string. In this picture the
boys are getting ready to make the shape of a kayak. It will take twenty-two separate
steps, but the boy's fingers will move quickly and it won't take them long. In all,
the people have over two hundred shapes to make and games to play with string.

ᓯᕐᓗᑦᑕᐱᕕᖕᖒᑦ   ᐊᖕᒍᒪᕐᖃᖏᑦ

ᐃᕝᓂ ᐊᕐᓇᒥ ᑕᑯᖕᓇᐅᕐᖅ ᐊᔭᖕᒥᑉᑖᓕ ᐃᒥᕐᒪᖕᒪᕐᖅ ᐅᐳᐅᑦ ᐊᔭᖕᒥᑉᑕᐅᑉ ᑕᐃᕐᒥᖃ
ᐃᓄᐃᑦ ᐊᐅᔭᖕᓂᑎᐅᓈᓐᑦ.   ᐊᕐᓈᖕᑦ ᖂᒥᕐᓇᑦ ᑕᖕᑦ ᓇᐅᐃᑦ,   ᐊᒪᕈᐅᑦ ᐃᕐᔪᓐᖒᓂᑦ ᖃᐅᓯᑦ
ᐱᑦᖃᖕᖏᑎᖒᓐᑦ ᕐᑕ. ᐃᓇᐃᑦ ᐱᑕᐅᕐᓈᓐᑉ ᐃᒥᒪᔭᐅᕐᖒᓐᑦ ᖄᖑᖒᑕᐅᕐᒥᕐᖕᖠ ᓄᕐᖅᑕᓂᖕᖒᓂᕐᖒᓐᑦ.

ᒥᖕᒍᖕᒍᑉᒍᖏᑯᖕ ᑖᓈᖅ ᐊᔭᖕᒥᑉᑕᐅᕐᖕᑦ ᖃᖄᖒᓕᑐᖕᓚᐅᕐᖒᖕᒪ ᐱᑦᖃᕈᓚᐅᕐᖒᖕᖔᖕᖠ, ᐅᐳᐅᖃ
ᐊᑕᐅᕐᕐᖒᑦ ᓇᓈᕈᓴᕐᒥᕐᖒᑦ ᖃᖏᕐᓚᖕᖒᓂᑦ ᐱᐊᖑᓴᖕᖒᓂᑦ ᐅᐳᐅᓚᐅᕐᖒᑦ ᐅᐳᐅᖕᖃᑐᖒᕐ.   ᑕᐃᒪ ᒪ̇ᓈᖃ
ᐱᕐᒪᕈᖔᕆᕐᖔ ᑐᕋᓐᑐᒥ.

Ancestral Hunters

This picture is about the woolly mammoth, thousands of years ago when the Inuit were not very tall. There was no caribou, no polar bear. There wasn't any wolf and there wasn't any dog. So the people have trapped a woolly mammoth in a pit and they are killing it, because there is nothing to eat. When I painted this woolly mammoth, I just knew it was there. Then, one year later, they found a frozen baby woolly mammoth from the Ice Age up in the Northwest Territories, and right now they have it here in Toronto.

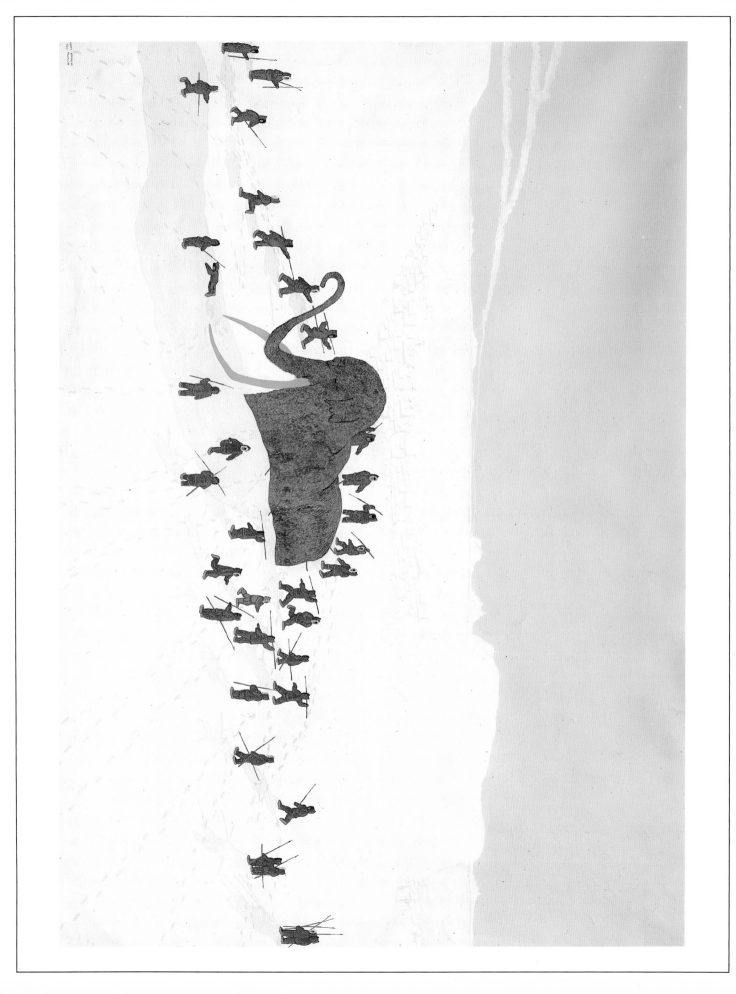

ᐊᕐᓇᕐᓱᐊᓄᐃᑦ ᐊᒻᒪᓗ ᖁᓕᓴᖅ

ᐊᕐᓇᕐᓱᔾ ᑕᑲᕐᓇᒋᒃ, ᐃᓕᖅᑕᓂᒃ ᑕᓄᐊ ᐊᕐᓇᕐᓱᒃ
ᐊᒻᒪᓗ ᑖᓇ ᐊᖏᖅᑕ ᐊᐃᕐᑕᐃᔭᕐᖕᒪᑕᕐᑦ, ᐊᕐᓇᕐᓱᕐ
ᑕᖃᓪᓇᖕᒃ ᐱᖏᖅᓇᑎᕐᓇᐊᕐᐅᓭᕐ ᐅᓂᓇᖃᒃᑕᖕᒃᑎᒐᕐᑦ
ᐃᓕᕐᑕᒐᖕᒃᒋᑕᖕᒃᓂᕐ.

ᐊᕐᓇᕐᓱᐊᓄᐃᒃ ᐊᖅ ᐱᖑᕐᕐᐱᖓᕐᖕᓇᒋᕐᑦ ᑕᓇᐃᕐᐃᑦᕐᑕᖕᒃᓇᕐ
ᐊᖁᓇᕐᒃᐸᖅᕐᑐᓄᕐᑦ.

Mermaids
and the Narwhal

We believe that just off Cape Jones, a long time ago, a father threw his daughter over the side of a boat. She was frightened and held on to the side of the boat. So her father cut off her fingers. She sank to the bottom of the water, where she became the Sedna, the sea goddess who is now a mermaid. All of the animals of the sea—the fish and the polar bear and the seal and the narwhal— were created from her cut-off fingers.

Sometimes it is dangerous in the water. A polar bear can swim out too far and then Sedna must help him back to shore. She cannot use her hands, because her fingers have been chopped off. Sedna uses her mind to make the animal turn back toward shore. The skin of the narwhal is soft and smooth. Sedna touches it and plays with it and rubs it. That is because the narwhal, who is like a king, is her son.

The mermaids will not bother people who go hunting on the sea. But if the people kill the wrong animal—anything that is on land, like wolf, fox, rabbit, ptarmigan—the mermaid will not help them. Because these people did the wrong thing, the mermaids could kill them if they wanted.

ART BY NORMAEE EKOMIAK.

ᐊᕐᕕᐃᑦᑐᕈᐅᐸᐸ ᐃᔅᓇ ᐊᖁᓄᖕᓕ
(ᐃᖅᑭᒥᓕᓂᖃᖦᒍ)

ᐃᓄᐃᑦ ᐅᖃᑎᒍᑦᖃᓕᓄᐱ, ᐊᐃᖦᖑᖕ ᐅᐸᐱᒃᖢᓕᓂᐱ
ᐊᒻᒪᓗ ᓇᖖᒃᐅᖅᖦᒃᖃᔪᓂᐱ ᓄᓇᒥᐅᑖᓄᒃ ᐃᓄᖦᑎᒥᒃᒐᒃᒃ
ᒦᐃᓄᓕᖦᐊᓐᖃᒃᐅᓂᑖᒃ, ᒦᓄ ᐊᑕᖁᓄ ᐃᓄᐊᒃ
ᐅᖕᖦᖦᐊᒃᑖᑐᐃᑦᑐᓄᖅᖦᓄᐱ ᐅᐱᒃᖖᖦᖦᖃᖁᓂᐱ, ᐅᖃᔅᐳᒐᒃ
ᐸᖦᐊᖃᐅᒃᐱᖕᓄᐱ, ᒥᖃᓐ ᐅᐸᐱᐅᒐᖦᐅᖦ ᓇᐱᖅᖦᑕᐊᖁᓄᒃᖖᖦ
ᒧᓄᐱᐃᒃᖁᓂᐱ.

Nativity (detail)

The Inuit are a very religious people. We have our own religion, and we worship the spirits of nature who protect us. At the same time, we are Roman Catholic or Anglican or Protestant or even Baha'i. I believe that what is in this picture is true.

ᒃᑕᐃᑎᑕᕐᑎᐃᑦ   ᐃᕐᓂᐊᕈᓂᐊᕐᖅ

[Inuktitut syllabic text]

Nativity

I believe that a Baby Jesus is born everywhere, to every different group of people in the world. Here Jesus is a baby Inuk. The people are bringing him their gifts, good luck charms: a narwhal tusk, a blanket, and a spear for hunting. The dog and the polar bear cub are there to watch over him and protect him.

Up in the sky the North Star and a great shooting star are signs of the miracle. Two snowy owls and two angels, with candles from the church, are there to watch and protect. The wolf on the hill is howling the good news to the moon, and it will be heard by more people, more children, and more wild animals, who will all come to Baby Jesus.

ᑕᐳᕐᑎᐅᑕ ᐱᓂᕐᖢ

ᑕᒐ ᒥᖁᓕᐊᕐᐸᕐᖅ ᓂᐱᖅᑯᕐᐅᓴᕐᐊᖅ ᑐᓂᕈᑎᐅᕐᖢᓴᑦ ᐅᖃᐅᓯᖃᕐᐊᒐᕐᓂᖅ ᐊᕐᐱᐊᔭᒍᑎᐅᒐᑕᑦ ᑕᒡᒍᒧᐱ
ᑕᐳᕐᑎᒍ 100-ᓂᖅ ᓇᓗᑎᐊᓐᖑᖅᖢ ᖃᓄᖅ. ᐊᐱᕐᑕᑎᑕ ᐸᑦ ᖃᒥᒃ ᓴᓐᕐᐊᕐ ᑕᒥᕐᖃᒍᑦ ᐊᕐᑕᐳᖅᑲᑐᑕᑦ
ᖃᓄᖅᑕᕐᑲᑕᑕ ᐊᒥᒐᐅᑦ ᐅᑭᐅᕐᐸᕐᖢ ᐅᕐᒪᐱᑕᒥᐅᕐᖁᖢᖅ ᒥᕐᖃᕐᑕᐳᖢᕐᓴᖅᑕᑕᑦ ᑕᐳᕐᑕᑎᖅ ᐊᖢᕐᖢ
ᕐᖢᐸᑕᐱᐊᓱᕐᐅᐸᕐ. ᑕᓴᓇ ᐅᑲᐱ ᖢᓴᕐ ᖃᒡᒐᑲᐱᐳᕐᖢᐊᕐᐅᑲ ᑕ ᖃᖅᑕᑕᐳᕐᖃᔭᓐᒐᑕᑦ, ᐅᐱᐳᑕᑕ ᐱᖃᐅᕐᐊᑕ ᐅᑕ
ᖅᖃᑕᐅᖅ ᐊᖢᕐᓴᖢᖃᑖᖃᑐᓂᑕᑦ.

The Spirit of Liberty

I made this wall hanging as a gift from the native people of North America when the Statue of Liberty was one hundred years old. The different-colored geese flying by stand for all of the races of man. They have all come to North America to enjoy liberty and happiness. Watching over them and the Statue of Liberty is Okpik, the spirit owl, who sees everywhere and who sees everything.

What I Have Done

In 1971, I had to leave Fort George. I was too lonely there. I could not always hear what people were saying but I knew they were laughing and pointing at me because of the sewing I used to do. So first I went to Ottawa to stay with my sister and her family. I did my art there and learned to eat some of the food of the south. I do not like to eat very much. I like to drink a lot of very hot, very sweet tea and I like to smoke cigarettes. When I have had a lot of tea and when there is a lot of smoke, then I can see the spirits and hear them. After, I went to live in Tottenham, near Barrie, Ontario, in a big house, with a man who had a very big garden. I showed which plants were special and were good. Then in 1972 I came to Toronto.

The Government paid for me to go to George Brown College. I learned how to do many things there. Then I went to work at a home for old people. But I only like doing my art and so I did not stay long at my job. In 1973, I worked at the Ontario Science Centre on the Inuit Cultural Exposition. The next year I was a guide at the Inuit Art Exhibit at the Toronto-Dominion Centre. After that, C.B.C. television asked me to design the costumes for a play about Inuit that was called *The Exe-cutioners* and was written by Farley Mowat, who knows the North and its people. Then in 1976, the Department of Indian and Northern Affairs paid for me to go to the New School of Art, in Toronto, to study. After that, I made many paintings and drawings and wall hangings which I sold to friends and to art galleries. I have had shows of my art in Toronto, in London, in Oshawa, in Ottawa, in Kapuskasing and in Barrie.

I tried to go back to Fort George but there is now a very big dam there for the Hydro-Quebec James Bay Project. Everything is under water and has been flooded. Many of the land animals were drowned and the nature spirits were not happy. But the government built a new settlement called Chisasibi, at the edge of the water where Fort George used to be. Now the fish and the sea animals and the birds and the land animals are starting to come back. But that part of the land was strange to me and so I came back to the South.

In 1986 I was the Official Native American Artist for the New York Statue of Liberty Foundation. I made a special wall hanging for the Museum of the American Indian. Then I was the representative of Canada at the International Children's Art Festival in New York. Back in Toronto, in London, in Kitchener and Waterloo and around Palgrave, the Ontario Arts Council pays me to go to the schools and to teach the children about the Inuit and to show them my art and to tell them all about me. I like the children in grades 4 to 7. They write me letters and say, "I think you are a perfect artist" and "You are a very good children entertainer" and they say "Your friend always." One special friend wrote me, "I liked your visit best when you told us about your walking in the air with your aunt."

I drink a lot of beer and people say I am an alcoholic. But the alcohol is good for me. When I look at a person on the street, I am always smiling. Those people look at me and they think I am sick. But sick is sadness and happy is always freedom. I get beaten up all of the time. Something is wrong with those other people but not with me. My scars are my souvenirs. Once I was beaten up so hard that I had to have an operation for my hearing. I cannot hear all of the people who laugh and who say bad things. But even here in the city, I can hear the owl and I can hear the bear, and the Sedna still sings to me.

Now I am forty years old. When I was young, a shaman told me I would live to be 80. I will not kill myself, because then the spirits will not be happy and I will not be able to go to heaven. So I will do my art and drink my tea and smoke cigarettes and listen to the spirits.

My North is not there any more. It is only in my memory. I live and work in the South. I am an Inuk of the city.

—*text prepared by Dr. Brian Dobbs*

THE PLATES